HARRY
at the Dentist

written by Ruby Nelson

Illustrated by Danny Noonan

The views and opinions expressed in this book are solely those of the author and do not reflect the views or opinions of the author.

Harry at the Dentist - Copyright © 2024 Ruby Nelson

ISBN: 978-1-922664-79-2 (Paperback) 978-1-922664-80-8 (Hardback)
All rights reserved. Neither this book nor any parts within it may be sold or reproduced in any format by any electronic or mechanical means, including information storage and retrieval systems without permission in writing from the author. The only exception is by a reviewer, who may quote short excerpts in a review.

"Today's the day, Harry! We're going to see Dr. Michael, the dentist. He'll make sure your teeth are sparkly and clean," said mom.

Harry grabbed his toothbrush and gave his teeth a beautiful clean. Round and round, up and down, front teeth and back teeth. They were sparkling clean. Harry was now ready for his dentist appointment.

Harry grabbed his teddy and they buckled in their seat-belts. He was a little nervous but Teddy held Harry's hand tightly and they were ready to go.

When they arrived at the dentist, Harry saw colorful toys, books and puzzles in the waiting room. He and Teddy found a beautiful red spaceship that was hidden in a box. "Woooosshhhh" said Harry as he flew the rocket around the room.

Dr. Michael came out with a big, friendly smile. "Hello, Harry! It's so nice to see you again!" Harry took a deep breath and held Teddy's paw.

"Just follow me Harry" as Dr. Michael pointed to a room down the corridor. "It's time to check your teeth".

"See that big chair?" Dr. Michael said.
"Hop on up"
Harry climbed into the chair, gripping the arms tightly. Up and down, backward and then forwards it tilted. It was like a rocket ship getting ready for take off. Harry loved it!

The dental nurse came over and gently placed a pair of glasses on Harry.
"Hi Harry. These will protect your eyes from the bright light," she said.
They are our special sunglasses just for the dentist.

Dr. Michael showed Harry some shiny tools. "These are just for looking at teeth," he explained. "They're like little helpers for me."

Harry stared at the tools, fascinated. There were long ones, short ones and even some with bendy ends.

"Alright, Harry, can you open wide like a lion?" asked Dr. Michael.

Harry opened his mouth as wide as he could, letting out a soft "roar."

Dr. Michael chuckled and started counting Harry's teeth one by one.

"You have such healthy teeth, Harry. Well done!"

Then, Dr. Michael picked up a small brush that buzzed like a bee. "This will make your teeth extra shiny," he explained. Harry watched in amazement as Dr. Michael gently polished each tooth. The buzzing tickled a little and Harry giggled.

Dr. Michael used his tools gently, Harry hardly felt a thing.
He grabbed some yellow tooth floss, that looked like some string.

Next, Dr. Michael handed Harry a small cup of green water. "Take a sip and give your mouth a big swish, then spit it into our little sink right here."

Harry took a sip and swirled the cool, minty water around his mouth before spitting it out.

"Great job, Harry" said Dr. Michael, giving him a thumbs-up.
"Your teeth look fantastic!"

"Just remember to keep brushing your teeth every morning after breakfast and every night before bed for 2 minutes. This will make sure your teeth stay strong and healthy".

Harry jumped down carefully from the chair, feeling proud and happy. See you in six months, Dr. Michael"

Dr. Michael handed Harry a brand-new toothbrush. "And here's a special toothbrush just for you, Harry."

With his teddy in one hand and his new toothbrush in the other, Harry grinned wide enough to show every single tooth. He skipped out of the room and it was so nice knowing his teeth were all healthy and clean.

HARRY'S
HEALTHY TEETH RULES

1. Brush your teeth twice per day. Once after breakfast and then following dinner.
2. Brush your teeth for 90 seconds. Make sure you brush your top teeth and bottom teeth both in front and behind and move your brush in big circles.
3. Avoid having drinks high in sugar like soda or juice poppers. Sugar can cause decay and form holes in your teeth. Water is the best drink to have!
4. Use a toothbrush with good bristles. Get a new toothbrush when the bristles begin to bend and get a new toothbrush every 3 months.
5. Visit your dentist every 6 months for a check-up. If your baby teeth are not healthy, this could hurt your adult teeth when they start to grow.

HARRY'S
Book Series

Available Via all Major Online Bookstores

www.ingramcontent.com/pod-product-compliance
Lightning Source LLC
LaVergne TN
LVHW072051060526
838200LV00061B/4709